THE MAD PAR
COUNTDOWN

John Poole
Southampton 7.4.90.

Illustrated by Mary Norman

JOHN MOLE

The Mad Parrot's Countdown

PETERLOO POETS

First published in 1990
by Peterloo Poets
2 Kelly Gardens, Calstock, Cornwall PL18 9SA

© 1990 by John Mole

All rights reserved. No part of this publication may be reproduced, stored in a retrieval system, or transmitted, in any form or by any means, electronic, mechanical, photocopying, recording or otherwise without the prior permission in writing of the publisher.

ISBN 1 871471 13 3

A CIP catalogue record for this book is available from the British Library.

Printed in Great Britain by
Latimer Trend & Company Ltd, Plymouth

ACKNOWLEDGEMENTS: some of the poems in this volume have previously appeared in the following collections by John Mole: *The Love Horse* (Morten), *A Partial Light* (Dent), *In and Out of the Apple* and *Homing* (Secker and Warburg).

Recipient of an Arts Council Incentive Funding Award

for
The Offley Gang

Contents

page
- 9 First Snow
- 10 A Ghost Story
- 11 Song for an Abandoned House
- 12 The Cry
- 13 The Classroom
- 14 A Painting Lesson
- 16 First Fruit
- 17 The Goldfish
- 18 Tell Me, Tell Me
- 19 The Joke
- 20 The Call
- 21 A Cradle Song
- 23 Bank Holiday
- 24 Circles and Squares
- 25 Three Cross Cat Rhymes
- 27 The Regretful Philosopher Apologises to his Cat
- 28 The Mad Parrot's Countdown
- 29 Bats
- 30 Sing a Song of Christmas
- 31 Asking for Trouble
- 32 Pig Sings
- 34 Why Did the Chicken?
- 35 Words of Advice from the King of Jazz
- 36 My Hero
- 38 Night Music
- 39 At the Top
- 41 Alice and Alice
- 42 Smug Jug
- 43 The Trick
- 44 Cinderella
- 45 from Penny Toys
- 51 Carnival Sunday
- 53 Moth
- 54 A Riddle
- 55 Good Night

First Snow

Whose is this long, unexpected elbow
Resting its white sleeve on the wall?
Is anyone out there when I call
To hear my voice? I've lost my echo.

Whose are those feathery tears that keep coming?
Somebody weeps without a sound
And leaves his grief heaped up on the ground.
It's so quiet my ears are drumming.

Whose is that handkerchief on the gatepost
Large enough for a giant sneeze?
Bless you whisper the shivering trees
While I just stand here like a ghost.

Who am I? And where have I woken?
It wasn't the same when I went to bed.
I still feel me inside my head
Though now a different language is spoken.

Suddenly all the meanings have gone.
Is someone trying to tell me something?
A bird shakes silver dust from its wing
And the sky goes on and on and on.

A Ghost Story

When you come home and it's raining
And there's nobody in
And the kettle's switched off but still steaming
And the biscuit tin
Is full of biscuits (your favourite kind)
And the beds have been made
And you look in the fridge and you find
Everything splendidly arrayed
For your best meal ever but when you call
Nobody answers and even the cat
(Who doesn't like rain) is not in the hall
Or the kitchen or upstairs or anywhere at all
And there's no message left on a table or the doormat
And the damp patch seems to have grown larger on the wall
Then you have to admit it at last—you're afraid
No not that they've gone and left you behind
But that you yourself have been delayed
And that somehow someone broke into your mind
Before you got home, that you'll have to begin
All over again, that you've woken from dreaming
And nothing has changed except nobody's in
(Not even the cat) and it's still raining.

Song for an Abandoned House

The glass is never mended,
The trees are always bare,
The sky is open-ended,
The end is open air,
The prospect is heart-broken,
The curtains will not close,
The truth remains unspoken,
The rest is not repose.

The rooms have been vacated,
The lock has turned its key,
The ghosts are reinstated,
The mirror cannot see,
The silence darts for cover,
The echo finds its voice,
The shadows haunt each other,
The house is spoilt for choice.

The Cry

Somebody started it.
Somebody must have.
Look at it this way,
You want to be somebody.
Somebody loves you.
Somebody must know.
Where is everybody?
How can nobody?
Surely somebody ...

Who needs anybody?

Somebody help!

The Classroom

Desk-lids deafen the dead with chaotic clatter,
Crisp-packets crackle and crinkle, a galaxy of gobstoppers
Glop and gurgle in cheeks blown big as bellies.
Stuck in a seat too small for his billowing bottom
Great George groans and the back row bellows with laughter.
A bundle of bags and books are hurled at a wimp called Wally
Who gawps then grunts then giggles until the bell goes.

But now it's midnight, and the school is silent,
The crisps have been crunched and the packets pulped by the cleaners.
A fierce face frowns from the blackboard, cheekily chalked up
By Great George. *Sir* it says in loopy lettering,
And the empty corridors echo with laughter.
Then the ghost of Wally's giggle goes to sleep until morning
As the very last lesson is left to the moonlight.

A Painting Lesson

(from the Studio of Benjamin Mole)

Henri de Toulouse Lautrec
Couldn't paint to save his neck—
'Bring me a model!' he'd exclaim,
Swigging brandy from his cane,
'One of those fagged-out, scrawny dollies
That kick their legs up at the Folies'.
Then he'd dash off a few quick strokes
(A habit with those famous blokes
Who're reckoned to be good at art
But never finish what they start)
And all his fans would say 'Bravo!
Go on, have another go'—
Which Henri did; he squeezed those tubes
And painted ladies with big boobs
And gentlemen with silly hats
And dogs which looked much more like cats
And posters for the Music Hall
(Lousy paintings one and all)
And no one told him 'They'd be nicer,
Henri, if they were PRECISER'
But *I'd* have told him, I'd have said
'Come on, Henri boy, instead
Of all those smears and dots and dashes
Get yourself some fine, thin brushes,
Get your models from the shelf
In a proper model shop—an elf,
An orc, an ogre or a dwarf,
A snotling, ratman, even a smurf
Would be far better than *your* type, oh
Why not try a Mutant Psycho;
Beastmen, Chaos Knights and dragons
Are much more interesting than flagons,
Coffee cups and knives and forks
And all that restaurant rubbish! Orcs
Are in and Paris out,

War Games are what it's all about,
Painting armour really neat—
So give yourself a birthday treat.
Buy me a model. Let's have some fun,
And watch me show you how it's done!'

First Fruit

Plucking a globe
From its living thread,
Light is orange
The painter said

Then considered this wasn't
For him to say,
Pocketed it
And walked away.

The Goldfish

Through the ice swept clear of snow
There suddenly appeared a glow,

A glow of orange, then a glower,
A gaping, vacant-featured flower,

A flower which floated up, a face
Against the limits of its space,

Its space I gazed at vacantly,
As distant as eternity,

Eternity, unnumbered years
Of thought which comes then disappears,

Then disappears, a guilty wish,
As quickly as that flowery fish,

That flowery fish which turned about,
Flickered, dimmed and then went out,

Went out like a fading light
Into the darkness, far from sight,

From sight, but never far from mind,
Leaving its after-glow behind,

Behind, before, just once, not twice,
No second glances through the ice.

Tell Me, Tell Me

Will you lead us up the path
If I can find your garden?
Shall I cry or will you laugh
When we beg each other's pardon?

If I become a rolling stone
Shall we gather moss together?
Will you be one and all alone
Or better late than never?

When you drop a stitch in time
Shall I be there to catch it?
If I close this heart of mine
Might you forget to latch it?

Shall we be proud before we fall
From our castles in the air?
Or do you hardly mind at all
And do I really care?

The Joke

What makes me laugh
Is when you start to tell a joke
And then forget it
Half-way through
So the joke becomes you,

Because you have always been
The biggest laugh
In my life;
It is you not doing anything by half-measure
That gives me such pleasure . . .

Like forgetting the joke
And saying *Anyway*
What does it matter anyway?
But have you
Heard the one about . . . ?

Then you forget that too.

The Call

You didn't answer when I called
Although I knew you must have heard.
Why was I suddenly appalled?
You didn't answer. When I called
The space between us was enthralled
And something in my memory stirred.
You didn't answer when I called
Although I knew you must have heard.

Why did you never call me back
Or let me know you'd changed the game?
Across our net's deceptive slack
Why did you never call me back?
Had I somehow lost the knack?
Were you really not to blame?
Why did you never call me back
Or let me know you'd changed the game?

A Cradle Song

(for Kieran)

Oh who is it hears
The moon when she cries
Or knows to what question
Love replies

Oh who is it shares
The grief of snow
Which whispers to come
But weeps to go

Oh who is it sees
The puzzled face
Of a world already
In disgrace

Oh who is it was
My own first name
As it now becomes yours
And is why you came

Bank Holiday

Far beyond the dingy pier,
The derricks and the dirty boats,
Water waves her ringlets, floats
In crystal cleanliness, cool, clear,
Calm and collected. As for us, we're
Sweating on this beach, our coats
Stretched out beside us, and our throats
As tight as terror, stiff as fear.

Oh for a coke, a ginger pop,
To touch our tongues, to lick our lips,
But all we do all day is flop
And long for breezy, tousled trips
Across the sea or dream one drop
That drips and drips and drips and drips.

Circles and Squares

Circles always meet themselves
At every turning of the way
On journeys that complete themselves
By never ending, greet themselves
Round corners then repeat themselves
Like questions. They

Are not those squares which frame themselves
From every angle that they make,
Which boastfully proclaim themselves
As always right, and name themselves
So shamelessly they shame themselves
But never notice their mistake.

Three Cross Cat Rhymes

as sung to its mistress by the cat in a famous painting

1.
Hey diddle diddle
I'll make your thumbs twiddle
If this painting is not finished soon:
I'm stuck here, sedate,
In a posture I hate,
As the dark tip of half a blue moon.

2.
Ding Dong Bell
Pussy's bored as hell.
You've kept me here for hours.
Why couldn't I be flowers?

3.
I love you, I love you,
Your coat is so warm
And you nestle your head
In the crook of my arm ...
Oh baloney and hogwash,
You don't half make me weep,
Why you're more of a softie
Than Little Bo Peep!

The Regretful Philosopher Apologises to his Cat

I consider the names I did not choose
Since a kitten could hardly be thought to have views
But, now that you've grown, your widening eyes
Dilate on a world of philosophies:
Cartesian cat, your purr in the sun
Is murmuring *Cogito ergo sum*
Or, Wittgenstein, your inscrutable face
Seems certain that everything is the case.
If this is an ideal home, you're Plato
Warming his paws in my study window
Then you make for the desk, transformed again
And, preferring the shade, become Montaigne.
When you're shut outside and it's raining hard
You look as gloomy as Kierkegaard
But on the tiles for a late-night razzle
You take hot tips from Bertie Russell.
Pensive at noon on a mellow brick wall
The secrets you keep would outblaise Pascal
Though you sometimes thump your tail, a feature
Which hints at the darker dreams of Nietzche.
Not least, with my garden to cultivate,
Voltaire might have suited, but it's all too late
As I call you in, to my lasting shame,
By your utterly commonplace cat name.

The Mad Parrot's Countdown

10   9   Wait (!)
Pieces of 8   pieces of 8
TERMINATE
7   6   Are you still alive
My hearties?   5
Gold rings   but listen I've
Learnt more
4
(Make Love not War)
3   2
It's down to you
Yo ho ho   Yo ho WHO (?)
1
Is 1
Is a bottle of rum
And ever more shall be so
Be so   be so
Be   ZERO ...

Bats

Bats like various
musty old areas:

belfries, of course,
where they rehearse

a crotchety score,
dangling galore

from cross-bar staves,
troubling graves

with the dark bells' boom
of their leather tune;

or a spooky loft
where dust lies soft

on forgotten things,
and someone sings

in her room below
that song bats know

whose notes contain
the squeak of pain . . .

Oh, bats like various
vicarious areas,

preferably precarious.

Sing a Song of Christmas

Sing a song of Christmas,
Sing a song of grub,
Sing a song of Grandpa
Boozing in the pub.

Sing a song of turkey,
Sing a song of sprout,
Sing a song of half past ten
And chucking Grandpa out.

Sing a song of brandy,
Sing a song of cheese,
Sing a song of big cigars
And Grandpa on his knees.

Asking for Trouble

I heard a warning voice today
And it didn't come from heaven;
'Just hang on
Till Sir has gone
And I'll duff you up!' said Kevin.

He poked a pencil down my neck
(The way his warning's given);
'Just hang around
Till we can't be found
And you'll be dead!' said Kevin.

I smiled, but no one saw me smile.
I know the odds are even.
'Just hang about
Till Sir nips out
And then ... Goodbye!' said Kevin.

What Kevin doesn't know I know
Is that today he's seven,
So I'll hang about, around and on
Then say 'You'd better watch it son,
But Happy Birthday, Kevin!'

Pig Sings

PIG'S SONG OF COURTSHIP

Grobble Snort
Blurp Blort
Screep Uggle
Slop Snuffle
Honk Squelch
Flubber Belch
Wee   Say
Wee   You
Wee   Love
Wee   Me

PIG'S FAVOURITE NURSERY RHYME

Sniff Piggle Piggle
Whiff Piggle Piggle
Truffle Tum Tum
    Tump
Glop Bubble Bubble
Up Bubble Bubble
Down Derry Derry
    Dump

PIG'S FOOTBALL CHANT

Blue Boar Kicks Mate
Who Wee Wee Appreciate?
P.I.G.
Pig!

PIG'S LULLABY

Trouble Sorrow
Dropple Wallow
Snort Snorkle Deep
Sadly Sobble
Cradle Wobble
Sleep Sleep Sleep

PIG'S FAREWELL

No Sow
Go Now

Why Did the Chicken?

Starting out across the road
The clever little chicken slowed
Then stopped. *I'm blowed*
It clucked *if I can see*
Why they should make a joke of me
And turned back, very sensibly.

Words of Advice from the King of Jazz

There ain't nothing worse
Than an old horn's curse.

When you try to sound slick
Them bent valves stick.

When you want to look cool
Your spit drips in a pool.

When you aim to impress
That lacquer's a mess.

When you need your tone thin
The mute won't go in.

When you're ready to shout
The mute won't come out.

But get a new horn
And, man, you're reborn.

My Hero

Marcel Proust's my hero,
Marcel Proust's my man.
I'll tell you why
Marcel's my guy
And I'm his biggest fan.

Marcel was a writer
Who wrote his books in bed,
And no one fussed
Or said *You must
Get up, Marcel.* Instead

His friends all came to see him
And brought him special cakes;
He'd take a bite
Then start to write,
Forget his pains and aches

And murmur *I remember* ...
The taste made him recall
A favourite game,
A flower's name,
The colour of a ball,

Until it all came pouring out.
Marcel was a *success*,
But still he lay
In bed all day
And didn't have to dress.

So that's why he's my hero—
There's homework to be done.
I didn't write
A word last night
And now the morning's come.

I'd like to lie here all day long
And try those special cakes;
I'm sure Marcel
Could count and spell
And not make bad mistakes.

Oh to be a genius,
Never to look a fool,
But best to stay
In bed all day
And not be missed at school.

Night Music

Hey diddle diddle
The Emperor's fiddle,
His soldiers are over the moon.
From andante legato
To mad pizzicato
Their wish runs away with his tune.

Where will it lead them?
He does not heed them—
Oh watch out for what music releases.
While your home is ablaze
The Emperor plays
Then leaves you to pick up the pieces.

At the Top

It was tough at the top but heady;
My friends made a pyramid—
Their tense arms juddered,
I gulped and shuddered
Supported by what they did.

I felt like the tower of Pisa,
I lurched like the Empire State,
But they stood their ground
While a groaning sound
Rose up from beneath my weight.

The nearer the earth you inhabit
The more you are bound to bear;
It's safer that way
But whatever they say
It was great at the top, and rare.

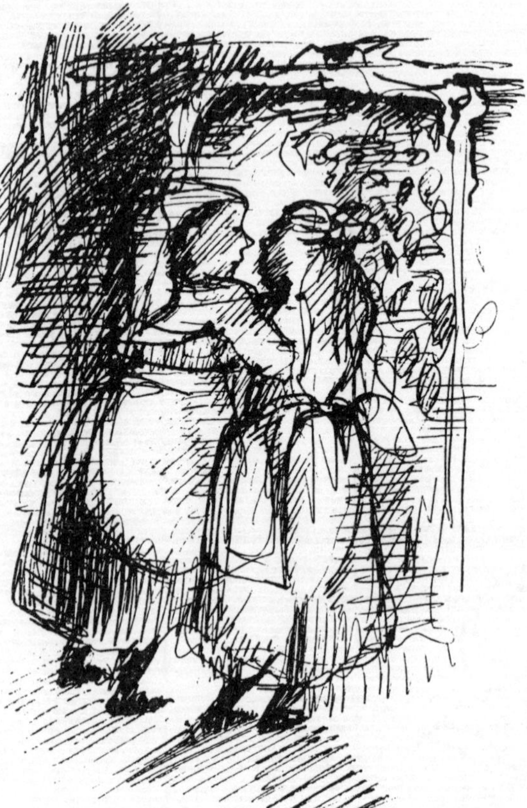

Alice and Alice

Arm in arm, Alice and Alice
Have walked through the mirror on the wall
And though neither of them is pretty at all
They are both of them nice.

They are going to teach the Queen some manners,
Nobody should behave like that,
And a hatter is no excuse for his hat.
They detest caterpillars.

A race is a race. Someone must win,
And beautiful soup is a matter of taste.
When a cynical cat dissolves with such haste
It should not leave its grin.

This time the sense will take care of the sound,
Language will banish the Jabberwock,
Minutes will do as they're told by the clock
And rabbits will stay underground.

Simply begin as you mean to go on.
If the Queen should cry *Off with her head!*
Alice and Alice are well enough bred
To know two are better than one.

Croquet is played with mallet and hoops,
Flamingoes aren't held by the leg.
If you're silly enough to try mending an egg
You won't need horses and troops.

The trouble with nonsense is that it's not true
Though the bottle says *Drink me who dares.*
Common sense walks like policemen in pairs
And reason stands to.

So Alice and Alice, arm in arm,
Whom nothing shall ever put asunder,
Have set out to vanquish the forces of wonder.
They mean no harm.

Smug Jug

Though caught in the act
Of admiring itself
For its porcelain tact,
Its high-on-the-shelf
Refusal to think
That someone might dare
Ask for a drink
When seeing it there,
This jug has just proved
That a proud heart takes pains
Not to be loved
For what it contains
While a heart that is true
Though mere earthenware
Is loved through and through
For what it can pour.

The Trick

One night, when I couldn't sleep,
My Dad said
Think of the tomatoes in the greenhouse

And I did.
It wasn't the same as counting sheep
Or anything like that.

It was just not being in my room forever
On a hot bed
Restless, turning and turning,

But out there, with the patient gaze of moonlight
Blessing each ripe skin
And our old zinc watering-can with its sprinkler,

Shining through a clear glass pane
Which slowly clouded over into
Drowsy, comfortable darkness

Till I woke and came downstairs to breakfast
Saying *Thank you, Dad,*
I thought of them. It did the trick.

Cinderella

It was something about
This pantomime
That puzzled me in
And out of time.

*Be back by midnight,
The spell can't last—*
No help from the orchestra
Or the cast.

My father holding
My mother's hand—
Why couldn't anyone
Understand?

When she reached the Ball
And danced with Prince Charming
I looked at my watch—
It's all right, darling,

It's only a story
My mother said
But the minutes ticked on
Inside my head

Until they were married,
The curtain fell,
And the future was left
To what time would tell.

from *Penny Toys*

CAT OF AGES

Cat of ages
Old and new
Let me hide myself
In you

Let me listen
Through your ears
To Adam's laughter
And Eve's tears

Let me gaze
On Pharaoh's tomb
Under a high
Egyptian moon

Let me feel
My whiskers twitch
Riding a broomstick
With your witch

Let me taste
Each salty morsel
Tossed by pirates
From the fo'c's'le

Let me smell
My supper cooking
And slip back home
When you're not looking

Cat of ages
How would it be
If you hid yourself
In me?

SAD GOOSE

Oh to be a swan—
I am much put upon!
Can no one transform me?
Is there no love can warm me?
Oh swan, my friend,
You will sing at the end
But I'm one of the low—
I shall just go.

THE MUSICAL MONKEY

The musical monkey is dressed like a flunkey
In bell-bottom trousers and little peaked cap;
His master the grinder could hardly be kinder
And everyone calls him an elegant chap.
But see how his face is a world of grimaces
Which might make us wonder and should give us pause;
Oh quaint little creature, oh great Mother Nature,
A dance for our penny, a fig for your laws.

WHAT DID THE PIG DO?

Well, there was this show
And they had me ready to go—
Scrubbed, shiny, pink,
All that wallow, all that stink
Clean gone. I was their prize
Porker. Some size, my friends, some size!

Worth my weight, they said—
A wallet stuffed with notes, and me dead—
One of those shows where you win
And lose. They do you in
With one hand and pay out with the other.
Oh brother, my friends, oh brother!

So I put my feet down, all four,
When they came to get me. No more
Mucking about. You can stick your knife
Up your ... It was *my* life
And I aimed to stay in it.
This was the limit, my friends, this was the limit!

No point being Number One
Is there, just to get done?
What I did—I leave you to guess.
There was *some* mess.
They were all thoroughly shaken
But it saved my bacon, my friends, it saved my bacon!

THE AIRMAN'S FAREWELL

Thanks for the spin. Don't prang the bus.
Scribbling and rhyme? No dice, old scout!
But we were the chaps. Remember us.
Willco. Roger. Over. Out.

I AM THE DOG

I am the dog whose master's voice
Lifted the hearts of an Island race.

I am the dog of pluck and grit.
Nobody tells me where to sit.

I am the dog whose brave bark reaches
Bedraggled troops on foreign beaches.

I am the dog no sausage hound
Is going to budge from his native ground.

I am the dog of World War Two.
Pray tell me, sir, whose dog are you?

SONG OF THE HAT-RAISING DOLL

I raise my hat
And lower it.
As I unwind
I slow a bit.
This life—
I make a go of it
But tick-tock time
I know of it.

Yes, tick-tock time
I know of it.
I fear the final
O of it,
But making
A brave show of it
I raise my hat
And lower it.

Carnival Sunday

On Carnival Sunday what could be finer
Than whanging a wellie and smashing china,

Than putting the boot in and splatting a rat
And drenching a burger with yukky tat,

Than buying old annuals you'll never read
And guessing the weight of a bear gone to seed,

Than quoiting a two-litre bottle of cola
And thumping a punch-bag which won't fall over,

Than stuffing your face until friends shout *That's gross!*
And then fungussing it with candy-floss,

Than paying 10p for a fist-full of darts
And splintering the wood round the ace of hearts,

Than junketing on an inflated castle
And not getting off when they blow the whistle,

Than watching two cars race round on a track
And cheering the one which skids onto its back,

Than raffling for a weekend in Paris for two
And wondering what, if you won, you would do,

Than finding a kid that has lost its mum
And telling the man with the microphone,

Then when it's all over what could be better
Than writing the whole world a thank-you letter?

Moth

Pity my silence pressing at your window
Frail and motionless against the night;
A baffled spectre framed by blackness,
Little moonflake, prisoner of glass.
This is my journey's end, receive me.
Brilliant keeper, rise and let me in.

Then later, when from a drawer perhaps
You take my body, wasted, brittle
As a shred of antique parchment, hold it
Gently up to the light I loved
But which bewildered me, until
I fly away again, a ghostly powder
Blown or shaken from your hand.

A Riddle

I am an instrument, a pipe,
A bright brass concertina
Making heavenly music.
Planets, spheres, the Plough, the Milky Way
All come at my calling
Winking at me, eye to eye,
As if they knew that he who plays me well
Will understand them, entering
The mystery of the universe and bringing closer
Infinite secrets held for aeons
In the darkness which I penetrate.

Play me in silence, and I'll give you
Silence in return
Though in your head, professor,
You'll be seeing stars.

Good Night

With one shoe on
And one shoe off,
The day's work done,
A bowl of broth,

I like it best
Just sitting here
Half at rest
And half at prayer.

The setting sun
A petalled rose,
The broth to come
Still warms my toes.

Whetting well
My appetite,
This sweetest morsel
Of the night

With one shoe off
And one shoe on,
A bowl of broth,
A simple song.

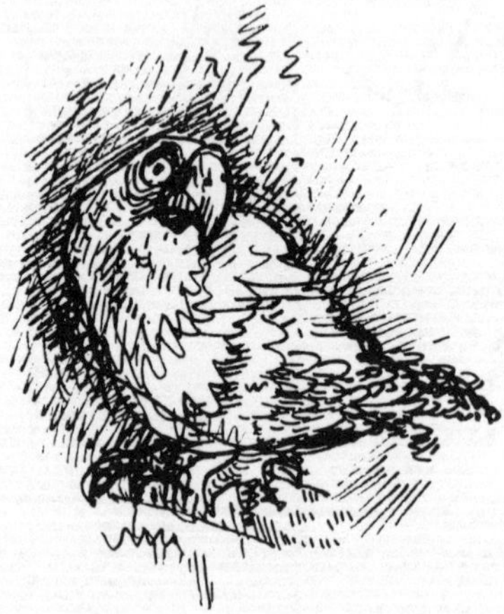